Original title:
Narrow Indents Amid the Elf Dub

Author: Olivia Orav
ISBN HARDBACK: 978-1-80563-360-0
ISBN PAPERBACK: 978-1-80564-881-9

The Enchantment of Luminous Trails

In twilight's grasp, the fairies play,
With glowing wings that light the way.
They dance upon the silver streams,
And weave the magic of our dreams.

A path adorned with sparkles bright,
Unfolds beneath the quiet night.
Each step reveals a hidden charm,
In this enchanted forest warm.

The stars above begin to sigh,
As moonbeams kiss the world nearby.
The trees hum soft, a lullaby,
Embracing all who wander by.

Upon the trails where shadows blend,
Mysteries start, and tales extend.
With every footfall, whispers call,
To hearts awaiting magic's thrall.

So let us roam where wonders gleam,
In lands where hope and joy redeem.
For in the dark, light's secrets dwell,
In every tale this night will tell.

Whispers of Lore in the Autumn Leaves

Beneath the boughs of fiery gold,
The tales of autumn softly unfold.
Each leaf a story, crisp and clear,
Of fleeting time that draws us near.

The winds carry secrets from afar,
Of harvest moons and evening stars.
They dance with glee in twilight's breeze,
Awakening the sleeping trees.

In twilight's glow, the shadows play,
Whispers of lore weave night and day.
With every rustle, a voice we hear,
Of dreams once lost, now drawing near.

Footsteps on the carpeted ground,
Echo the magic all around.
As twilight fades and darkness creeps,
The forest hums as the world sleeps.

So gather 'round, and hear the call,
Of ancient tales that still enthrall.
For in the leaves, the truth resides,
In autumn's grasp, where hope abides.

Beneath the Boughs of Forgotten Lore

In the woods where whispers dwell,
Memories weave a secret spell.
Beneath the boughs, the stories sleep,
Guardians old, their vows to keep.

Ancient roots, with wisdom bind,
Echoes of the past entwined.
Each rustling leaf, a tale retold,
Of brave hearts, and dreams of gold.

The moonlight dances on the glade,
Where shadows stir, and magic's made.
In twilight's grasp, the dreams take flight,
A realm of wonder, void of fright.

Through tangled vines and flowing streams,
Adventure calls in silver beams.
Kindred spirits, hand in hand,
Explore the realms of this enchanted land.

A Journey Through the Veil of Shadows

On paths where twilight softly falls,
A journey starts as silence calls.
Through veils of shadows, whispers wane,
Lost hopes and fears, a hidden pain.

Stars above, a distant guide,
As restless hearts in shadows glide.
Each step a tale, and breath a song,
In the night, where dreams belong.

Flickering lights, like fireflies,
Illuminate the midnight skies.
With every choice, the spirits sway,
Through dusk and dawn, they guide the way.

The veil grows thin, with every tread,
In twilight's arms, where fears are shed.
The journey's wild, but filled with grace,
You'll find yourself in this quiet space.

Fables from the Silent Grove

In the heart of a silent grove,
Where ancient trees with secrets strove.
Fables born from whispered leaves,
In every breeze, a tale believes.

From silver streams where shadows play,
The tales of yore begin to sway.
Imagined worlds in each soft cheer,
Adventure waits for those who hear.

Voices of the past entwined,
Within the grove, a truth aligned.
Each rustling branch, a lesson shared,
With gentle hearts, the brave have dared.

In stillness blooms a wondrous lore,
Awake the spirit, seek and explore.
In fables found beneath the trees,
The soul ignites with every breeze.

Echoing Footfalls on the Mossy Path

On mossy paths where echoes dance,
Each footfall sings a sweet romance.
A melody of ages past,
With every step, the die is cast.

Beneath the arch of leafy shade,
A hidden world in silence laid.
Where whispers chase the fleeting light,
And shadows weave through day and night.

The ancient stones, in quiet pride,
Bear witness to those who abide.
In gentle curves, the journey flows,
As magic stirs where no one knows.

With spirit bold, the heart should roam,
For mossy paths lead always home.
In every thread of time's embrace,
Find echoing footfalls, grace in space.

Ashen Spirits in the Moon's Glow

In shadows deep, where secrets lie,
The ashen spirits whisper nigh.
With silver light, they softly tread,
Under the gaze of the silent spread.

They dance anew in twilight's call,
Their murmurs echoing through the hall.
Of ancient tales and lost delights,
They weave their magic through the nights.

With every breath, the night ignites,
As dreams take flight amidst the heights.
They swirl around in ghostly grace,
A fleeting glimpse of their embrace.

In moonlit realms, they find their peace,
Where time stands still and sorrows cease.
They beckon forth the brave and bold,
To share their stories, dark and old.

So linger not, but heed the call,
Where ashen spirits weave through all.
In twilight's heart, their truths reside,
In moon's soft glow, they gently glide.

Echoes of Laughter in the Hollow

In verdant glades where laughter rings,
The echoes dance on fleeting wings.
A gentle breeze through branches sways,
Remembers joy in sunlit days.

Each whispers soft like morning dew,
The magic of the moments new.
In every rustle, in every sigh,
The hollow hums where spirits fly.

With hearts entwined in shared delight,
They weave their tales through day and night.
With every chuckle, in every cheer,
The world around mirrors what is dear.

So gather close, let joy take flight,
In laughter's arms, we find our light.
In every nook, the warmth remains,
An endless echo that sustains.

Embrace the bliss, let worries part,
For in this hollow beats a heart.
In shared delight, our souls entwine,
In laughter's song, we truly shine.

Whispers of the Elders in the Thicket

In tangled woods where shadows dwell,
The elders speak, their tales compel.
With wisdom laced in every tone,
In whispered words, their truth is sown.

Through ancient roots and leafy spires,
Their stories spark like hidden fires.
They guide the lost, they soothe the meek,
With tender voices, soft yet sleek.

In twilight's gloom, they share their lore,
Of days gone by and so much more.
With every breeze that stirs the leaves,
Their gentle hearts, the forest weaves.

So listen close, to what they say,
In rustling leaves, the past's ballet.
For in the thicket, wisdom grows,
A timeless bond each spirit knows.

Through winding paths, where echoes cling,
The elders teach what life can bring.
In every whisper, courage finds,
A thread that ties all tender minds.

Fantasies Woven by Twinkling Stars

Beneath the vast, enchanted night,
The stars weave dreams in silver light.
With every twinkle, stories bloom,
In cosmic dance, dispelling gloom.

They sparkle bright in velvet skies,
A tapestry before our eyes.
Each sparkle holds a tale so grand,
Of worlds unseen, at fate's command.

In dreams we chase what hearts desire,
As fantasies ignite the fire.
In whispered hopes, they spark the flame,
In unity, we share their name.

So close your eyes, let visions soar,
The stars will guide to distant shores.
In every glance, some magic stirs,
A universe that gently whirs.

With every wish upon a star,
Believe in dreams, no matter how far.
For in the night, we find our way,
In fantasies that brightly play.

A Tapestry of Echoes in the Underbrush

Whispers weave through tangled leaves,
Each secret carried on a breeze.
Beneath the boughs where shadows creep,
Ancient lore, in silence, sleeps.

Footfalls soft on mossy ground,
A symphony of life around.
The rustle of a hidden sprite,
Guides the moon's soft silver light.

Here in the thicket, dreams revive,
In the heart of green, we come alive.
Mysteries dance in twilight's glow,
As nature's song begins to flow.

Echoes ring, like bells of yore,
Unraveled tales from days before.
Each flicker of a lantern's flame,
Ignites the world, and calls our name.

So wander deep in realms of old,
Where stories rich and wild unfold.
In every twist of winding path,
Lies the magic and quiet wrath.

Radiance in the Realm of Enchanted Beings

In twilight's grasp, the fairies gleam,
Their laughter weaves a silver dream.
Beneath the canopy of stars,
Magic pulses, near and far.

With wings that shimmer, glint, and soar,
They dance on petals, evermore.
Each flicker bright, a fleeting spark,
Illuminates the hidden dark.

Amid the trees, a symphony,
Of whispers soft and harmony.
The nightingale, a bard so wise,
Sings of wonder 'neath the skies.

In glades adorned with nature's grace,
The fae entwine, a warm embrace.
Together, they spin stories bright,
Of hope and joy, of day and night.

So linger here, let spirits twine,
As realms unseen begin to shine.
In this enchanted space, we find,
Reflections of the heart and mind.

The Fae's Lair: Whimsy Entwined with Nature

Beneath the blooms where moonbeams play,
The fae have made their hideaway.
In verdant shades, they weave delight,
With laughter pure as morning light.

A dais made of dewdrop gems,
Where joy erupts like woodland stems.
Each whispered wish upon the air,
Can paint the world with magic rare.

In every nook, a tale unfolds,
As meadows hum with whispers bold.
The colors swirl in vibrant dance,
Inviting hearts to take a chance.

Among the leaves, the sprites reside,
With friendly grins that cannot hide.
A wink, a nod, then off they go,
To spread their whimsy, fast and slow.

So follow paths where laughter's clear,
In spots where wishes draw you near.
Embrace the magic in the air,
For whimsy thrives in nature's care.

Shadows Playing in the Glimmering Glade

In the glade where shadows meet,
Mysteries whisper, soft and sweet.
Glimmers dance on silver streams,
Awakening the world of dreams.

Night unfolds with gentle grace,
Embracing all in dark embrace.
The stars like jewels overhead,
Light secrets where the brave have tread.

Amongst the ferns and tangled bark,
There lies a magic, bright and stark.
The echoes of the nightingale,
Lead souls to where the tales prevail.

With every rustle, each faint sigh,
The shadows shift, as spirits fly.
They call us forth to realms unknown,
To dance where light and dark have grown.

So venture near, in dusky hue,
To where old souls weave something new.
In this glimmering glade of lore,
The heart finds peace, forevermore.

Realms of Wonder Under the Midnight Sky

In realms where dreams take flight,
Beneath the shimmering night,
Whispers of magic weave,
In tales that none believe.

Stars like lanterns softly glow,
Guiding lost souls in the flow,
A dance of shadows, sweet and sly,
In realms of wonder, we learn to fly.

Moonbeams sprinkle paths of gold,
Secrets of the night unfold,
With every step, a new delight,
Awakening hearts in the moonlight.

The breeze carries stories untold,
Of brave adventures, fierce and bold,
Each rustle speaks of worlds unknown,
In midnight realms, we find our home.

So sit you down, embrace the dream,
In starry skies where starlights gleam,
Together we'll chase the endless sigh,
Exploring wonders under the sky.

The Guardian's Song in the Night

Beneath the cloak of twilight's grace,
A guardian keeps a watchful place,
With eyes like embers, bright and keen,
Protecting realms that lie unseen.

As shadows stretch and silence reigns,
The guardian sings of ancient chains,
A melody that weaves the air,
Enchanting all who stop and stare.

Through rustling leaves and brimming streams,
The song embraces all our dreams,
In every note, a promise lies,
Awakening hope beneath the skies.

When fears creep close and darkness looms,
The guardian's song dispels the glooms,
With every chord, a brightening light,
Guiding lost hearts through the night.

So heed the whispers of the song,
For in its echoes, we belong,
In melodies that gently sway,
The guardian keeps our fears at bay.

Lurking Magic Within Fern Fronds

In shadows deep where ferns do grow,
A magic stirs, a secret flow,
With emerald arms, they twist and glide,
Holding whispers of the tide.

Each frond a tale, a life concealed,
In verdant depths, the heart revealed,
Gentle breezes brush the leaves,
Bearing tales that nature weaves.

In morning light, they gleam like gems,
A world alive with faerie hems,
Delicate, fragile, yet so grand,
Lurking magic at our hand.

So wander close, and take your time,
In ferny realms where wonders chime,
Listen close, let your spirit soar,
For magic hides forevermore.

With every step, feel nature's beat,
In whispered songs, we are complete,
Through ferns we learn to dance and play,
In the magic found along our way.

Wandering Spirits Beneath the Stars

In moonlit fields where shadows dance,
Wandering spirits take their chance,
To roam the night in playful glee,
Embracing all that's wild and free.

With hearts that flutter, soft and light,
They weave through darkness, a wondrous sight,
Each pulse a story, each laugh a song,
In the embrace of the night so long.

Stars gaze down with knowing eyes,
As spirits whisper of their ties,
To worlds unknown and dreams untold,
In the hush of night, their stories unfold.

Through valleys deep and mountains high,
They chase the echoes of the sky,
In every twinkle, every spark,
A path of magic, bright and dark.

So join the wanderers in their quest,
To find the peace, the heart's true rest,
For beneath the stars, we come alive,
In the embrace of magic, we thrive.

The Dance of Shadows on Velvet Leaves

In the hush of twilight's grace,
Shadows dance, a fleeting trace.
Velvet leaves in moonlight sigh,
Whispers soft as breezes fly.

Figures swirl in shadowed light,
Murmurs tease the edge of night.
Nature's waltz in gentle flow,
Guiding dreams where soft winds blow.

Stars above begin to gleam,
Casting magic on the stream.
Magic weaves through night's embrace,
Every flicker holds a face.

In this tapestry of dark,
Every flicker leaves a mark.
Echoes of the day's delight,
Resting softly, out of sight.

Veils of night with secrets bind,
Layers deep in gentle kind.
In the dance of shadows cast,
Timeless tales from ages past.

Mysteries Woven with Stardust Threads

In the fabric of the night,
Stardust weaves with threads of light.
Mysteries of time untold,
In the heavens' grasp, behold.

Whispers spin in cosmic trails,
Echoes of forgotten tales.
Galaxies in quiet dance,
Each a story, each a chance.

Celestial hands write and fold,
In the darkness, dreams unfold.
Every twinkle, every gleam,
Holds a fragment of a dream.

Through the void, the heart will soar,
Seeking treasures evermore.
Navigating through the vast,
Holding tight to love amassed.

Mysteries in silence drape,
Crafting hopes, the heart's escape.
Such is life, a wondrous thread,
Woven tight where stardust led.

Faint Glows Through Leafy Canopies

Faint glows flicker, shy and bright,
Through the leaves in cloak of night.
Whispers drift on velvet air,
Nature's song, a tender prayer.

Canopies of emerald veil,
Guarding secrets none can pale.
Every shadow tells a tale,
Of forgotten dreams that sail.

Tiny lights begin to hum,
In the dark, their voices come.
Mingling with the breeze's sigh,
Glimmers spark as stars drift by.

Rustling leaves in gentle sway,
Guide the night along its way.
Every heartbeat softly plays,
In the glow of moonlit gaze.

Softly now, the night unfolds,
As the world around it holds.
Faint glows shimmer through the trees,
Carrying the night's sweet breeze.

Dreams Whispered to the Otherworld

In the twilight, dreams take flight,
Whispers soft like stars at night.
Carrying hopes to realms afar,
Beneath the watchful evening star.

Voices from the otherworld call,
Gentle echoes, rise and fall.
In the silence, truth is found,
Magic dances all around.

Every sigh a tale to weave,
Lost in shadows, dreams believe.
Paths of wonder in the dark,
Light a fire, breathe a spark.

Winds of fate begin to spin,
Whispers in, and then within.
Carried forth by breaths unseen,
Guiding hearts through realms between.

So let dreams be gently sown,
In the fields where thoughts have grown.
Whispers sweet will always guide,
To the otherworld, dreams abide.

Echoes of Mischief Beneath the Foliage

In shadows deep, where secrets creep,
The woodland whispers tales to keep.
Fleeting forms dance in disguise,
Mischievous glimmers in emerald eyes.

Beneath the boughs, laughter rings bright,
Twinkling stars in the velvety night.
The trickster's game, with a wink and a grin,
Invites all hearts to join in the spin.

With every rustle, a story unfolds,
Of bold little spirits, daring and bold.
Through tangled paths, destinies twine,
In the echo of mischief, eternity shines.

Hidden beneath the thick leafy crown,
Little feet scamper, never to drown.
The forest, alive with tales to explore,
Holds mysteries waiting forevermore.

So come tread softly, wear laughter like a cloak,
Among playful shadows where magic awoke.
For in every echo, each giggle and cheer,
Lies a spark of enchantment, forever near.

Veils of Myth in the Twilight Realm

As twilight descends, the world gently sighs,
Veils of soft mist cloak the night skies.
Whispers of lore drift like feathers,
Entwined in the dance of enchanted heathers.

Beneath the gaze of the moon's tender light,
Legends awaken, woven from night.
Chasing the stars, with tales yet untold,
Veils lift softly, revealing the bold.

Each shadowed corner, a secret awaits,
Carving the dreams where wonder abates.
In echoes of legends, we find our way,
Through the twilight realm, where spirits play.

The air thick with magic, like honey sweet,
Inviting the curious hearts to repeat.
A waltz with the fairies, a heartfelt embrace,
Within the myths of this timeless space.

So wander beneath, the veils wrapped tight,
Where the fabric of worlds blurs your sight.
In the twilight's glow, belong you shall,
To the realm of myths where nightbirds call.

The Hidden Path of the Woodland Fae

In whispering woods, where mysteries bloom,
The fae weave spells with the scent of perfume.
Crickets serenade beneath towering trees,
Guiding lost souls on a soft, gentle breeze.

A path made of moonbeams, shimmering bright,
Leads you through gardens of starlit delight.
Glowing with secrets, the air lightly hums,
As laughter of faeries playfully strums.

Each footstep a ripple in murmuring streams,
The echoes of laughter entwined with your dreams.
They flicker like fireflies, cheeky and bold,
Telling old tales that the forest holds.

Through thickets and thorns, with petals to pave,
Adventures await in the heart of the brave.
The hidden path beckons, your heartbeats align,
To dance with the fae through the branches that twine.

So follow the flickers, the twinkles that call,
To the whispering woods where enchantments enthrall.
In the heart of the forest, with fae you will meld,
On the hidden path, your spirit upheld.

Intricate Trails of the Forest's Heart

Through intricate trails, the whispers lead on,
Where roots intertwine 'neath the sky's gentle dawn.
Every shadow a fragment of stories once told,
Of creatures and wonders, both timid and bold.

The gnarled branches form a canopy high,
Like guardians of secrets that shimmer and sigh.
Dappled sunlight dances on leaves far above,
A tapestry woven from nature's pure love.

Eager footsteps tread on the path ever winding,
With each twist and turn, new mysteries finding.
Though the forest may shift, its heart stays the same,
In the pulse of the woods, we are part of the game.

With the rustle of foliage, stories ignite,
Of lost dreams and hope, flickering bright.
The queries of life call, come wander and roam,
In the intricate trails, you might find your home.

So let curiosity guide your dear heart,
Through the forest's embrace, let adventure start.
In the labyrinth of green, where laughter departs,
Lie the intricate trails of the forest's heart.

Twilight Echoes Beneath the Canopy

In quiet woods where shadows play,
The whispering leaves greet the fading day.
Silence dances on the breeze,
As twilight wraps the world with ease.

The deer moves softly through the gloam,
While fireflies weave their flickering dome.
That gentle hush, a beckoning call,
To secrets hidden, both great and small.

Mossy stones hold stories untold,
Ancient magic in the twilight unfold.
Beneath the branches, hearts take flight,
In the dimming glow of stolen light.

A chorus of crickets plays with pride,
As the moon tiptoes, a silver guide.
Each rustle and murmur a song so sweet,
In the canopy where wonders meet.

With every step, the night unfolds,
Enchanted realms and destinies bold.
A journey deep through the fragrant glade,
Where dreams emerge and fears are laid.

Enchanted Paths and Tangled Trails

Through winding woods where magic dwells,
Where stories breathe and silence swells.
Paths intertwine, a tapestry grand,
With secrets waiting, like grains of sand.

The brook sings softly, a silver thread,
As ivy weaves a blanket of dread.
Each twist and turn a riddle to seek,
With whispers of wonder in every creek.

Beneath the oak, the faery rings bloom,
Inviting souls to dance in their gloom.
A flicker of hope in the shadowed deep,
Where dreams unfurl and longings seep.

Honeyed laughter floats on the air,
As starlit trails lead to realms rare.
Each footfall an echo of tales once spun,
In the enchanted glow of the setting sun.

The scent of pine and lavender's grace,
Awakens the heart to a mystical place.
On enchanted paths, adventure awaits,
As destiny opens its myriad gates.

The Lure of the Faery Meadows

In fields where the wildflowers sway,
The faeries come out to dance and play.
With laughter bright as the morning light,
In meadows adorned with colors so bright.

Petals whisper secrets, soft and low,
Underneath the sun's warm glow.
A world of charm, where shadows blend,
And every moment feels like a friend.

The brook nearby sings a lullaby sweet,
Inviting all to take a seat.
Where dreams take flight on a gentle breeze,
Amidst the blooms and tall, swaying trees.

With every sigh, the meadows call,
Enticing hearts, enchanting all.
A glimpse of magic in the simplest things,
A love that dances on silken wings.

In faery meadows, the heart can roam,
Finding solace, feeling at home.
Where the promise of joy is forever near,
And the laughter of faeries is all we hear.

Under the Starlit Veil of Dreams

Beneath the arch of a velvet sky,
Where twinkling stars like whispers lie.
A world awakens in the quiet night,
Wrapped in the glow of celestial light.

The moon casts shadows that gently weave,
Stories and dreams for those who believe.
With every sigh, the stars ignite,
A tapestry of wonder, pure delight.

In the hush of night, wishes take flight,
Dancing on beams of silver and light.
Each flicker a promise, a glimmer of hope,
Binding souls with an ethereal rope.

The nightingale sings a haunting refrain,
Filling the air with joy and pain.
A lullaby wrapped in soft embrace,
Guiding the dreamers to a magical place.

Under the starlit veil, dreams come alive,
A realm where the heart is free to strive.
With each twinkle of light to pave the way,
Into the wonders of night's ballet.

Secrets Spun in Gossamer Threads

In twilight's hush, where secrets dwell,
A web of whispers starts to swell.
The moonlight bends, a silken trace,
Of dreams that float in soft embrace.

With every shimmer, stories weave,
Of hidden realms that few believe.
Through eyes of stars, they gently peep,
Into the shadows, dark and deep.

A tapestry of fate aligns,
Unraveling the mystic signs.
In fervent heartbeats, magic sings,
As time unwinds on whispering wings.

The gossamer threads, so finely spun,
Link every soul, the many, the one.
Together we dance in this twilight glow,
Where secrets bloom and spirits flow.

Awaken now, in silence tread,
For every dream is delicately bred.
And in the stillness, hear the sound,
Of gossamer threads that tightly bound.

A Dance Among the Whispering Pines

Beneath the boughs where shadows play,
The pines sigh soft, in twilight's sway.
A whispered song, the breezes send,
Inviting all that dare to blend.

With every sway, the branches hum,
A melody from realms to come.
In nature's arms, rejoice and twirl,
With secrets held and magic swirl.

The dance unfolds, with steps so light,
In starlit paths, we find our flight.
Let laughter ring through forest green,
As echoes weave where we have been.

In hidden groves, we twine and spin,
As night descends, the dreams begin.
With every turn, the world awakes,
In whispered trust, our spirit breaks.

Together we'll weave our story bright,
Beneath the pines and soft moonlight.
With hearts entwined, we joyously dine,
In a dance among the whispering pines.

Glimmers of Magic in the Mist

As dawn unfolds in veils of gray,
The mist, it curls, begins to play.
With ghostly whispers, secrets sigh,
Where glimmers of magic softly lie.

In every drop of dew's embrace,
There lingers life, a fleeting trace.
With wonder's spark, the world ignites,
As shadows shift in morning's lights.

The trees, they dance, in silence bold,
Their stories told in bright and gold.
Through veils of vapor, dreams take flight,
In every breath, a spark of light.

With each soft step, the air will hum,
To ancient tunes, the heart will thrum.
In endless cycles, tales unfold,
Of magic found, of wonders told.

So linger, dear, in morning's grace,
For in the mist, you'll find your place.
The glimmers twine, like threads of fate,
In whispers soft, the magic waits.

The Hidden Language of Sylvan Beings

In emerald depths where shadows lie,
The sylvan beings softly sigh.
They speak in rustles, leaves a-flutter,
A hidden tongue that makes hearts shudder.

With every breeze, they share their lore,
Of ancient trees and legends more.
Through whispered roots, their wisdom flows,
In every glade, their spirit grows.

A language laced in bark and stone,
In harmony, we are not alone.
The forest breathes, we breathe in time,
In sacred rhythms, pure and sublime.

With eyes wide open, we can find,
The pulse of nature intertwined.
Each fluttering leaf, each bending bow,
Shares secrets that the heart can know.

So wander deep where silence weaves,
And listen close to what believe.
The hidden words can shape and guide,
As sylvan beings walk beside.

Whispers in the Hollow Grove

In the hollow grove, where whispers dwell,
A tapestry woven of magic's spell.
The trees stand tall, with secrets to share,
As moonlight glimmers on the cool night air.

Beneath the boughs, the shadows play,
While crickets chirp their nighttime ballet.
An owl hoots softly, wise and aloof,
Guarding the dreams of the forest's youth.

With every breeze, the leaves would sigh,
Echoes of stories that never die.
A world unseen, where fairies tread,
Filling the air with words unsaid.

The brook hums low, a gentle tune,
As starlit skies embrace the moon.
In this hollow, time slips away,
Where magic lingers, night and day.

So listen close, dear heart, take heed,
Among the whispers, the wild things breed.
For in this grove, all is enthralled,
And the spirit of wonder ever called.

Shadows Dance in Enchanted Glades

In enchanted glades where shadows dance,
The flickering lights seem to entrance.
Flowers bloom in a riot of hues,
Beneath the watchful gaze of the muses.

Moonbeams spill on the forest floor,
Whispers of magic, an ancient lore.
Echoes of laughter, sweet and clear,
As creatures gather, drawing near.

Ferns wave gently, they sway and bend,
As night draws near, the dark descends.
A breeze carries tales of old,
Of bravery, adventure, and hearts of gold.

In the heart of the glade, a firefly's glow,
Guides the lost souls through twilight's show.
Their flickering dance, a beckoning light,
In shadows that cradle the spirit of night.

So wander, dear dreamer, and lose your fear,
In the sway of the glades, magic's near.
For with each step, a new tale awaits,
In shadows that dance, where wonder resonates.

Secrets of the Moonlit Thicket

In the thicket where moonlight spills,
Secrets unravel, and mystery thrills.
The silver beams touch the wildflower's crest,
A sanctuary where the heart finds rest.

Moss carpets the path, soft and deep,
Where the guardians of the night quietly keep.
Beneath the branches, old stories ignite,
Awakening whispers in the still of night.

Echoes of fae on whispers glide,
Painting the shadows where secrets abide.
With every rustle, new tales are spun,
As the moon reigns high, watching over the fun.

Each glance through the leaves reveals hidden sights,
A glimpse of an age where magic ignites.
As silverfish dance on the water's edge,
The thicket blooms under night's gentle pledge.

So linger a while, let the wonders unfold,
In the thicket's embrace, warmth against the cold.
For in every secret, a truth will arise,
Beneath the moon's never-fading eyes.

Flickers of Light in the Woodland Mist

In the woodland mist, where magic weaves,
Flickers of light dance among the leaves.
A symphony plays between tangled roots,
As twinkling orbs lead the way through shoots.

The fog wraps close, a silken shawl,
Hiding secrets in twilight's thrall.
Ancient trees whisper, their voices blend,
With the murmurs of time, they twist and bend.

Starry-eyed dreams find their way home,
As fireflies flit through the forest's dome.
Every glow tells a story bold,
Of nights wrapped in silver, and ages old.

So step lightly, dear soul, as you tread,
In the woodland's heart where the shadows spread.
For in the enchantment, the mysteries rise,
Flickers of magic beneath starry skies.

The mist enfolds, a soft, sweet sigh,
As night enfolds the world nearby.
In every whisper and radiant gleam,
Lies the essence of every deeply held dream.

The Path Less Traveled by Tiny Feet.

In twilight's glow, a trail unfolds,
With secrets kept and tales untold.
Tiny feet dance on the mossy floor,
Where whispers of magic beckon to explore.

Beneath the arch of ancient trees,
The air is laced with mysteries.
Every step a spark ignites,
In shadows dim, where wonder lights.

The lantern bugs flit on the breeze,
As laughter mingles with the leaves.
Paths diverge, yet hearts align,
In this enchanted world, so divine.

With every turn, a vision bright,
Dreams take wing in the velvet night.
A melody sweet, a siren's call,
To journey forth, to rise, to fall.

For those who wander, those who roam,
The path less traveled leads us home.
In every step, a tale unfurled,
A journey through a spellbound world.

Whispers in the Woodland

Beneath the canopy bold and wide,
Where gentle creatures choose to hide,
A symphony of whispers flows,
In hidden nooks where magic grows.

Leaves murmur secrets, ancient lore,
With every breeze, they ask for more.
The elder trees with arms outstretched,
Guard tales of yore, their roots enetched.

Colors dance where fairies play,
In glimmers of gold and shades of gray.
A sprite flits past with a wink and grin,
Chasing the echoes that softly spin.

Among the ferns, a stillness deep,
Where shadows play and daydreams sleep.
The woodland's heart beats soft and slow,
In tranquil waves that gently flow.

With every rustle, every sigh,
The woodland whispers gently, "Why?"
To listen close, to let hearts mend,
In nature's arms, the weary blend.

Secrets of the Hidden Grove

In a grove where silence reigns supreme,
Where sunlight filters through a dream,
Secrets nestle in the roots,
Of ancient trees with leafy suits.

The air is thick with magic's breath,
As if the grove could trap its depth.
Little creatures glimpse and hide,
In shadows where the whispers bide.

Each flower blooms with tales to tell,
Of fleeting time and casting spells.
Petals flutter with a knowing grace,
In this enchanted, hidden space.

A brook murmurs softly to the stones,
Secrets shared in gentle tones.
Yet listening in this secret place,
Reveals the heart's most sacred face.

With every rustle of the leaves,
The hidden grove your spirit cleaves.
Embrace the magic, embrace the glow,
In this sacred space, let your dreams flow.

Shadows of the Pixie Glade

In twilight's hush, the pixies twirl,
Around the hues of twilight pearl.
Their laughter floats on soft moonlight,
Turning shadows into flight.

The glade begins to softly hum,
With secrets born from twilight's drum.
Tiny wings whisper through the trees,
A melody carried by the breeze.

In the corners where shadows meet,
They weave their magic, light and sweet.
A dance of dreams, a spark of glee,
In every flicker, wild and free.

The night reveals a wonderland,
Where tiny hands weave tales grand.
In the glade where laughter blooms,
The heart finds home amid the glooms.

So linger long in the pixie light,
Where shadows dance and spirits take flight.
For in this glade where dreams are made,
The magic lives in every shade.

The Heartbeat of the Shimmering Woods

In the shadows where secrets weave,
The trees whisper softly, and softly believe.
With rustling leaves that dance in the light,
The heartbeat of nature, a curious sight.

Crickets serenade the cool evening air,
While fireflies twinkle, a magical flare.
The brook gurgles stories of ages gone by,
As starlight drips gently from the night sky.

Mossy carpets cushion each wandering foot,
A realm where enchantment takes root.
With every step, a tale is spun,
In the shimmering woods, where dreams run.

So linger and listen, let your heart race,
Every heartbeat echoed in this sacred space.
For here in the woods, where wonder ignites,
The magic persists through the softest of nights.

The ground hums a rhythm, steady and true,
Awakening spirits, both old and new.
In the shimmering woods, time seems to bend,
To the heartbeat of nature, forever my friend.

Lullabies of the Moonlit Fables

Under a veil of silver so bright,
The moon casts enchantments, a soothing light.
Whispers of fables drift through the trees,
Carried by breezes, like soft, gentle pleas.

Stars twinkle high, a celestial choir,
Each note of their songs fuels heart's desire.
Dreamers are cradled in night's sweet embrace,
Lost in the wonder, in time and space.

In the arms of the night, shadows take flight,
Tales unfold softly, like dreams in the night.
The owls murmur secrets in riddled rhymes,
While magic is stitched in the fabric of times.

The rivers reflect the moon's sleepy face,
Flowing with stories of each hidden place.
As twilight unfolds in a silvery hue,
The lullabies beckon, inviting the new.

So come, dear listener, and let your heart roam,
For in every fable, you'll find a home.
In the cradle of night, where futures embrace,
The moonlight sings softly, a wondrous place.

Heartstrings of the Elfin Heart

In the glen where the fairies twirl and play,
The heartstrings of elves weave night into day.
With laughter like music, they flit through the air,
Their joy is a treasure, so splendid and rare.

Each note from their lyres ignites the still night,
Painting the darkness with colors so bright.
A tapestry spun of laughter and song,
In the heart of the elfin, where treasures belong.

Their dances are whispers, light as a sigh,
Inviting the stars to join in the sky.
For every heartstring is strummed with delight,
Creating a symphony, pure and so bright.

Among the tall trees where the shadows blend,
Magic is summoned, where pathways ascend.
With every heart shared, a flicker ignites,
In the heart of the elfin, love always invites.

So listen intently, let the music flow,
Through valleys and hills, let your spirit glow.
For in each gentle note, a story imparts,
The heartstrings of wonder, the elfin heart.

Curiosities in the Midst of Secrets

In a world where mysteries twine and entwine,
Curiosities beckon, and hearts intertwine.
Beneath ancient trees, whispers begin,
A labyrinth spun from the secrets within.

Dust motes dance freely in sunbeams so bright,
Guiding lost wanderers through shadows and light.
Every corner holds echoes of ages untold,
With secrets that shimmer like diamonds and gold.

Riddles abound where the wildflowers grow,
Veils of the past hide the tales that we know.
With each whispered promise, a path to explore,
Curiosities linger at every door.

Beneath velvet skies, where the old souls reside,
The forest confides all that it cannot hide.
So seek for the wonders that name cannot claim,
For secrets are treasures, and curiosities flame.

Unlock every door with a heart full of quest,
The thrill of discovery is always the best.
In the midst of secrets, let your spirit soar,
For curiosities beckon, forevermore.

Threads of Light Beneath Ancient Boughs

In shadows deep where whispers dwell,
The ancient trees weave stories well.
Their roots entangled, secrets bound,
In threads of light, lost hopes are found.

Beneath the boughs where dreams take flight,
The dance of time, a gentle sight.
With every breeze, a tale anew,
Each rustling leaf, a voice so true.

The sunbeams peek, a playful tease,
As nature sings, the heart's unease.
A tapestry of emerald hue,
Where magic swirls, and dreams accrue.

In twilight's soft, embracing glow,
The forest holds its secrets low.
With every branch, a story spun,
Of battles lost and victories won.

So wander here, where shadows play,
And let your soul find its own way.
For threads of light beneath these trees,
Are whispers sweet upon the breeze.

Where Time Meets the Enchanted Stream

Along the bank where waters shine,
The flow of time is intertwined.
With ripples soft, they sing their song,
In harmony where dreams belong.

Each stone embedded holds its tale,
Of journeys vast, of hope's frail sail.
Beneath the bridge where shadows play,
The echoes of the past will stay.

The silver fish that dart and weave,
Invite the heart to dare believe.
In sparkling depths, the secrets gleam,
Where time meets with the enchanted dream.

The willow sways with gentle grace,
Embracing all who find their place.
And in its shade, by stream's embrace,
A whisper stirs the tranquil space.

So let the current draw you near,
To find the truth, to face your fear.
For in that moment, pure and bright,
You'll grasp the world in threads of light.

The Lantern's Glow in the Thicket

In thicket dense where shadows creep,
A glimmer calls from dreams half-sleep.
The lantern's glow, a guiding spark,
Illuminates the boundless dark.

With flickering flame, it dances high,
Shedding warmth 'neath the midnight sky.
Each flicker holds a story told,
Of whispers hushed and hearts so bold.

The path unfolds through tangled vines,
Where nature's art in silence shines.
And every step is woven tight,
With hope that ties the day to night.

In circles wide, the echoes swell,
As dreams embark, where shadows dwell.
The lantern sways in rhythm slow,
A heart's desire, a fervent glow.

So chase the light, beyond the thorns,
Embrace the night, and greet the morn.
For in the thicket, spirits sing,
By lantern's glow, all life takes wing.

Murmurs of the Forest's Heart

In every rustle, whispers rise,
The forest speaks beneath the skies.
Its heartbeat pulses, soft and deep,
In ancient tones, in secrets steep.

The brook does laugh, the winds do sigh,
In nature's tongue, the truths comply.
Each branch that sways, each flower blooms,
A testament to life that looms.

With every dusk, the magic swells,
In shadows cast, the story dwells.
The owl's call, the crickets' song,
In concert grand where all belong.

Beneath the boughs, old tales revive,
As spirits dance, the forest thrives.
In whispered tales that time imparts,
You'll find the pulse of nature's heart.

So wander forth where echoes play,
And let the woods your spirit sway.
For in these depths, where secrets part,
You'll hear the murmurs of the heart.

The Melody of the Shimmering Stream

In the hush of dawn's first light,
Rippling whispers tease the night,
Each droplet sings a sweet refrain,
As silver sparkles weave their chain.

Beneath the willows, shadows dance,
With every twist, a fleeting chance,
To catch a glimpse of dreams anew,
In waters deep, a world to view.

The gentle current tells a tale,
Of heartbeats soft and breaths inhale,
Where secrets hide in every bend,
And laughter's echoes never end.

When twilight's brush paints skies afire,
The stream's sweet song will never tire,
For in this place, where moments gleam,
Life flows on like a wisping dream.

So linger here, let time be still,
Embrace the flow, let hearts be filled,
With melodies, serene and bright,
A shimmering stream of pure delight.

Secrets Shared with the Night Birds

In the silence of the dusky hour,
Whispers drift from leaves and flower,
As night birds gather, tales unfold,
Secrets shared in hushes bold.

Beneath the stars, a crescent moon,
They serenade the night in tune,
With feathered hearts, they sing their truth,
Of timeless wonders, lost in youth.

In the shadows, magic weaves,
Through melodies the darkness leaves,
A chorus ringing soft and clear,
To wrap the world in love sincere.

The rustling trees lean close to hear,
Each note a promise, drawing near,
While dreams take flight on wings of night,
In secrets shared, all feels just right.

So listen well, as echoes soar,
The night birds sing of days before,
Their hidden truths, like starlit skies,
Will always guide where hope will rise.

Glade of Lost Dreams and Forgotten Tales

In the glade where shadows creep,
Old echoes sigh, and silence weeps,
Once vibrant thoughts now softly fade,
In whispers soft, the past parades.

Beneath the branches, tangled tight,
Stories linger in waning light,
Of dreams that danced on breezes bold,
Forgotten gems, their worth untold.

Each fallen leaf a tale to share,
Adventures caught in autumn's snare,
As time slips by with gentle grace,
Memories bask in nature's embrace.

But here in this enchanted wood,
Where silence blooms, and hope once stood,
Dreams lie waiting, soft and still,
To weave anew, if hearts but will.

So seek the glade where spirits sigh,
With open minds and watchful eye,
For in lost dreams, new paths await,
In forgotten tales, we find our fate.

The Cradle of Twilight's Embrace

In the cradle where twilight glows,
Whispers weave through blooming rows,
As day drifts softly into night,
Hearts awaken 'neath fading light.

Velvet skies stretch wide and bold,
Embracing dreams that dare take hold,
While stars begin their twinkling song,
Guiding the lost where they belong.

In murmurs soft, the shadows sigh,
As night unfolds its blanket nigh,
With memories wrapped in tender care,
Each breath a promise, light as air.

Through the dusk, enchantments sway,
Painting hopes in hues of gray,
Where spirits dance in gentle trance,
A fortune found in twilight's glance.

So rest your heart and close your eyes,
In twilight's cradle, let love rise,
For in this space, where magic weaves,
Life's sweetest dreams and peace believes.

Whimsies of the Dreaming Glade

In the glade where shadows play,
Whispers weave through dusk and day.
Mushrooms dance beneath the trees,
Carried gently on the breeze.

Glittering lights like firefly dreams,
Paint the air with shimmering beams.
A brook sings softly, sweet and low,
Tales of magic, long ago.

Find the secrets in the mist,
Where the twilight fairies twist.
Underneath the willow's hue,
Life's enchantments bloom anew.

Giggles twirl in joy abound,
In this hidden, sacred ground.
Every leaf a whispered song,
In the glade, where dreams belong.

Beneath the Canopy of Starlit Wishes

Beneath the stars, so vast and bright,
Wishes flutter through the night.
Constellations spin their tales,
Sending hope on silken sails.

The moon, a guardian of dreams,
Bathes the world in silver streams.
Nightbirds sing their lullabies,
While magic twinkles in our eyes.

Dewdrops gather on the grass,
Reflecting dreams that softly pass.
Every shadow holds a spark,
Illuminate the endless dark.

Crickets play their serenade,
In this shimmering, starlit glade.
Each heartbeat, like a gentle wish,
With the stars, our hearts enmesh.

Enigma of the Woodland Spirits

In whispers low, the spirits dwell,
Guardians of the forest well.
Branches sway, their laughter shy,
Echoing the softest sigh.

A flicker here, a shadow there,
Secrets float upon the air.
Roots entwine like stories told,
Of ancient paths and treasures old.

Through tangled brambles, light breaks through,
O'er the rocks, the water's blue.
Feathered friends with soaring grace,
Guide our steps through this safe space.

The spirits whisper in the trees,
Carrying the wanderer's pleas.
In the depths of emerald night,
Their laughter glimmers, pure delight.

Delicate Drifts of Moonlit Ferns

In twilight's kiss, the ferns arise,
Underneath the starlit skies.
With gentle grace, they sway and bend,
Delicate drifts that seem to blend.

Moonlight weaves a ghostly thread,
Cocooning dreams in azure bed.
Each frond unfurls with whispers rare,
Inviting magic's tender care.

Softest shadows claim the ground,
As the world whispers all around.
Every shimmer holds a tale,
Of ancient woods and midnight gale.

Nature's breath, a calming balm,
In moonlit ferns, a world so calm.
Let us wander through this night,
Where dreams take flight in gentle light.

Murmurs of Magic in the Leafy Shadows

In the hush of the woods, whispers creep,
Where ancient secrets in silence sleep.
Leaves dance softly, the wind's gentle tune,
A realm of wonder beneath a silver moon.

Twilight spills gold on emerald blades,
Fairies flit in the woven glades.
Each flutter a spark, each giggle a sigh,
In the magic of dusk, on a night so spry.

Moss carpets paths where dreams entwine,
With soft glowing lanterns, the night is divine.
Echoes of laughter ring through the trees,
A symphony played on a whispered breeze.

Old oaks stand tall, guardians wise,
Their branches entwined, a web of skies.
In their shade, the enchantments abound,
In shadows that cradle the secrets unbound.

As night deepens dark, a chorus begins,
The stories of magic, where every heart wins.
Murmurs of joy sway with the leaves,
In the heart of the wild, where the world believes.

The Twilight Gathering of Elfin Souls

As the sun dips low, a gathering starts,
Elfin souls weave in with delicate arts.
In twilight's embrace, where shadows unite,
They dance in circles, their laughter takes flight.

Silver threads flicker like stars 'bove the ground,
Each whispered incantation, a magic profound.
With eyes like the forests, aglow in the night,
They cradle the dreams that begin with the light.

Beneath ancient boughs, a soft music swells,
Secrets entwined in the soft, gentle bells.
Branches sway gently, in rhythm they nod,
As starlit voices weave tales from the sod.

A trickle of laughter, a shimmer of glee,
Elves sharing stories, just as they please.
With promises whispered like leaves in the breeze,
In twilight's embrace, all worries can cease.

When the moon graces sky, through shadows they glide,
Together they dance, their hearts open wide.
Each step on the grass leaves a glimmering trace,
A treasure of moments in time's warm embrace.

As dawn starts to break, they fade with the light,
Then linger in dreams, till the day meets the night.
Elfin souls gathered, forever they'll dream,
In the twilight's sweet magic, a shimmering gleam.

Threads of Enchantment in the Dappled Light

In meadows adorned by the sun's gentle rays,
Are splashes of color that dance through the haze.
A tapestry woven of magic and grace,
In the dappled light, all shadows embrace.

With flowers that laugh and rivers that sing,
The threads of enchantment each blossom can bring.
From petals to streams, where fairies play,
In a world built of dreams, where wishes hold sway.

Hush now the whispers, let stillness prevail,
For magic resides in each breeze that sets sail.
A flicker of wings, a glimmer of light,
Threads weaving stories, hearts shining bright.

So gather the stardust, let joy unfold,
In the warmth of the sun, let adventures be told.
With laughter like music, and joy on the breeze,
In the gentle embrace of the rustling trees.

As twilight descends, the enchantments grow bold,
The secrets of night, like stories retold.
In the dappled light's warmth, our spirits take flight,
Finding treasures of wonder, deep into the night.

And when morning awakes, we'll return once more,
To the threads of enchantment, past our dreams' door.
In every petal, in every sweet chirp,
Magic's gentle touch, in our hearts left to stir.

Unseen Realms in the Verdant Maze

Through the thicket and brush, where mysteries dwell,
Unseen realms of wonder weave stories to tell.
In the heart of the wild, where the wild things play,
Whispers of magic guide us on our way.

Hushed are the echoes within leafy lanes,
The soft rustle sings of forgotten names.
With each turn and fork, the path opens wide,
Revealing the secrets where marvels abide.

Flickers of shadow dance in the dusk,
With scents of the earth, in the air, a sweet musk.
Mysteries woven in each silver ray,
Guiding the lost through the verdant array.

Creatures of legend peep round each tree,
With eyes like the twilight, wild and free.
In the maze of the green, their laughter resounds,
In the hush of the night, where enchantment abounds.

With every deep breath, we join in the song,
As we wander the realms where the heart can belong.
In the whispers of leaves, through the moon's gentle
beam,
We'll find our own magic, where the world meets a
dream.

And when morning arrives, with kisses of light,
The unseen realms fade, but oh, what a sight!
In the verdant maze, where the wonders lie,
We'll carry the magic beneath each bright sky.

Threads of Twilight in Sylvan Realms

In twilight's weave the shadows play,
Where whispers drift on leaves of gray.
Beneath the boughs, the secrets sigh,
As twilight threads the evening sky.

The ancient trees, with wisdom rare,
Stand sentinel, their roots laid bare.
A tapestry of dusk unfolds,
In amber hues and tales retold.

Fireflies dance in gentle pools,
Their light a guide, as silence rules.
The nightingale begins her tune,
Her melody a soft cocoon.

Yet in this peace, a mystery,
Woven tight like destiny.
For in these woods, the heart can roam,
And find within a whispered home.

So linger here, in twilight's hand,
Where dreams are spun from starlit sand.
Each thread a wish, each wish a spark,
In sylvan realms, we'll leave our mark.

Enigmas of the Emerald Depths

In depths where emerald shadows bloom,
Enigmas rise from nature's womb.
The glow of secrets softly glints,
In rivulets where magic hints.

Beneath the waves, the fae reside,
With laughter echoing like the tide.
They weave their tales in silken streams,
And wrap the world in verdant dreams.

The currents whisper ancient lore,
Of sunken ships and lost rapport.
In every ripple, stories churn,
While lighthouses from the shadows learn.

So dive into this liquid glow,
Where wonders wait, with ebb and flow.
The depths reveal what hearts may seek,
With every turn, a voice unique.

In emerald hues, the night unfolds,
A tapestry of secrets told.
Enigmas dance where few have tread,
In twilight's perfume, dreams are fed.

Shadows of Laughter Amidst Ancient Oaks

Beneath the ancient oaks so grand,
Where whispers twine like lovers' hands.
Shadows laugh in dappled light,
Holding secrets of the night.

Each gnarled root, a story spun,
Of missed connections, tried and done.
While branches sway in gentle jest,
A legacy of joy expressed.

The cool breeze carries giggles near,
A playful dance, a chorus clear.
In every rustle, tales entwined,
Echoes of laughter left behind.

Let not the weight of time erase,
The spirit of this sacred space.
For in the shadows, treasures bloom,
Amidst the woodland's fragrant loom.

So treasure laughter's fleeting flight,
Embrace the joy that sparks the night.
In ancient oaks, with shadows bold,
We find the warmth of tales retold.

Songs of the Wandering Breeze

The wandering breeze sings soft and low,
A melody that starts to flow.
It dances through the fields of gold,
A lullaby of stories told.

It carries whispers from the trees,
A fragrant dream on summer's breeze.
With every gust, the world awakes,
As nature joins in joyful takes.

Each note that flutters on the air,
Brings moments kissed with tender care.
From mountains high to valleys deep,
The breeze, a promise, sweet and steep.

So let your spirit ride the gale,
In every shimmer, find the trail.
The songs will guide you through the day,
In every heart, they long to stay.

As twilight calls and stars arise,
The breeze will weave through midnight skies.
A serenade of hope and peace,
In every sigh, our joys increase.

Elfin Laughter at Dusk

In twilight's grasp, the secrets dance,
Elfin laughter sings of chance.
The shadows twirl beneath the trees,
As magic whispers on the breeze.

With silver tones the night descends,
Where starlit paths and wonders blend.
In every sparkle, dreams ignite,
Elves revel, banishing the night.

Through glades adorned with vibrant hues,
They weave their songs, the softest muse.
And as the day gives way to night,
The world aglow with pure delight.

Each giggle flows like gentle streams,
A melody that stirs our dreams.
Caught in the spell of dusk's embrace,
We find our hearts in this enchanted place.

So linger here, let worries fade,
In elfin laughter, joy is made.
For in this realm where shadows play,
We dance together until break of day.

Veils of Mist and Moonlight

Beneath a curtain of soft mist,
The moonlight weaves a silver tryst.
Each soft glow hides a tale untold,
In whispers where the night unfolds.

The ancient trees stand tall and wise,
Guardians 'neath the starry skies.
With every rustle, secrets swell,
And in their shade, the shadows dwell.

A path entwined with evening's breath,
Leads onward, facing dreams or death.
With every step, the heart takes flight,
In veils of mist, we lose the light.

The echoes call through midnight's veil,
Summoning tales of quests and trails.
As moonbeams dance on dew-kissed ground,
A magic deep within is found.

So wander lost, let shadows play,
In dreams where hopes and fears can sway.
For in this veiled and mystic night,
The world unfolds, and hearts take flight.

Tales from the Eldritch Hollow

In Eldritch Hollow, where shadows grow,
Tales of mystery softly flow.
With every breeze that stirs the air,
Whispers of magic beckon, rare.

Through twisted vines and ancient stone,
Legends linger, never alone.
Each footstep echoes dreams long past,
In the hollow, time creeps fast.

From moonlit glades to haunted glens,
The spirits watch as daylight ends.
With eyes aglow, they share their lore,
Inviting seekers to explore.

In twilight's grip, the stories bloom,
Filling the air like sweet perfume.
For every shadow, a tale begins,
Where light retreats, and magic spins.

So wander deep through this sacred place,
Embrace the wonders time will trace.
For in the heart of Eldritch lore,
Adventure waits forevermore.

Flickers of Hope in the Twilight

When twilight drapes the world in gold,
A flicker of hope begins to unfold.
With every dusk, a promise gleams,
Awakening the heart's lost dreams.

In whispers soft, the stars ignite,
Guiding lost souls through the night.
Each shining orb a beacon bright,
A signal that we'll win this fight.

Through shadows deep, our spirits soar,
With every step, we seek for more.
The path ahead may twist and turn,
Yet in our hearts, the fire will burn.

So let the darkness fade away,
For dawn holds dreams, not far away.
In flickers of light, we find our way,
The promise bright of a brand new day.

And as the night starts to retreat,
Remember love is bittersweet.
For in each flicker, hope will thrive,
Guiding us forth, forever alive.

Pathways Woven by Gossamer Creatures

In twilight's hush, the fairy's flight,
Weaves magic threads in silver light.
Upon the leaves, soft shadows play,
Guiding the lost along their way.

A spiral dance of earth and air,
With whispers sweet, beyond compare.
Each dewdrop holds a hidden dream,
A world where light and kindness beam.

Through tangled woods, their laughter sings,
Of ancient tales and hidden wings.
With every step, a story's spun,
Beneath the gaze of the setting sun.

Where blossoms bloom and starlit skies,
Reflect the wonders in their eyes.
The gossamer trails lead hearts anew,
To realms where hope and joy break through.

The Silent Song of Rooted Dreams

Beneath the earth, where shadows dwell,
The whispered dreams weave potent spells.
In every root, a story lies,
Of daring hearts and starlit skies.

The ancient trees stand tall and wise,
With secrets held beneath their guise.
They listen close, in silence deep,
To wishes made, to promises keep.

In autumn's chill, the leaves will fall,
A rustling hymn, an echo's call.
Yet deep within, the pulse remains,
Of life reborn through winter rains.

And when the spring's embrace arrives,
In vibrant hues, the spirit thrives.
From every seed, a hope will spread,
In rooted dreams, where light is fed.

Dancing Sparks Among Whispering Leaves

When dusk descends, and shadows creep,
The forest wakes from evening sleep.
With flickering lights, the sprites come near,
Their laughter bright, a song we hear.

Through branches bent, and starlit paths,
They twirl and spin in joyful wraths.
A gentle breeze, a soft embrace,
As nature sways in mystic grace.

With every hop and graceful leap,
The night awakens, no longer deep.
Each glowing spark is a tale to tell,
Of night's enchantments in a spell.

And when the dawn begins to break,
The whispers fade, the stillness wakes.
Yet in our hearts, the dance remains,
A treasured memory of wild refrains.

The Veil Between Worlds in Nature's Embrace

In twilight's glow, where dreams take flight,
A veil descends to cloak the night.
Among the ferns, secrets abound,
In nature's arms, solace is found.

The river's song, a soft caress,
In every ripple, time's duress.
Each hidden nook, a doorway wide,
Where magic waits, and hearts abide.

Through whispered winds, the echoes blend,
Of worlds unseen, where journeys end.
A tender touch of ages past,
In nature's weave, our fates are cast.

With every step through verdant shrouds,
The spirit soars, the heart enclouds.
To wander where the wild things roam,
In troubles lost, we find our home.

Twilight Whispers of a Forgotten Realm

In twilight's glow, the shadows wane,
Whispers rise from the ancient lane.
Every stone tells a tale untold,
Of secrets buried, of dreams of old.

The twilight hums a lullaby sweet,
As stars awaken from slumber's heat.
With every breath of the night's embrace,
Time dances lightly, a fleeting trace.

In foggy mist, the past draws near,
A spectral laugh, a muffled cheer.
Forgotten voices fill the air,
In realms where magic lingers there.

The trees sway gently, swathe the ground,
In their deep roots, old magic found.
Echoes whisper from long ago,
In twilight's realm, the shadows glow.

Beneath the moon, a silver thread,
Weaves through the dreams where few have tread.
In whispered shades both dark and light,
A world awaits beyond the night.

Echoes of Giggles in the Forest Path

Down the winding forest trail,
Laughter dances on a gentle gale.
Each step a spark of spirit free,
In nature's heart, sweet jubilee.

Sunbeams filter through leafy crowns,
Chasing away the darkest frowns.
With every giggle, the world anew,
A melody crafted for me and you.

In dappled light where shadows play,
Children's laughter leads the way.
Whimsical echoes, a playful tune,
Beneath the watchful gaze of the moon.

Frogs croon softly, joining in,
While flowers sway in a whimsical spin.
The forest whispers ancient lore,
A world of wonder, forevermore.

Twisting paths of emerald hue,
Invite the heart to dance anew.
Each echo lifts the spirit high,
As time slips gently, passing by.

Wisps of Light Dancing on the Breeze

In the twilight air, soft lights collide,
Glimmers of magic a-wash with pride.
Wisps of laughter, twinkling bright,
Softly they weave through the velvet night.

Beneath grand oaks, they weave and twirl,
A festival cast in a luminous swirl.
With every flicker, a tale unfolds,
Of dreamy nights and starlit folds.

Gentle winds whisper secrets rare,
Carrying wishes, spreading care.
Each breath of air holds a chance to dream,
In this twilight realm where wonders gleam.

Through ancient glades, the shadows creep,
Where magic stirs and dreams run deep.
With every flutter, reality bends,
As wisps of light draw near like friends.

Stars above nod to the dance,
Lending their glow to every glance.
In the soft embrace of balmy zest,
The world is glowing, at its best.

Unveiling Secrets of the Enchanted Night

In the heart of night where shadows play,
Mysteries linger, secrets sway.
With every star that lights the dome,
Whispers call us to find our home.

Beneath the veil of a moonlit shroud,
The hush of night holds a pulsing crowd.
Each breath a promise, a silent vow,
To unveil the magic that lies right now.

Through twisted paths and hidden glades,
Curiosity's fire never fades.
In every rustle, a tale resounds,
Of ancient magic that still surrounds.

The forest sighs and the stars will gleam,
Every shadow a forgotten dream.
With each heartbeat, the night unfurls,
A tapestry woven of starlit pearls.

As dawn approaches, the secrets sway,
In the light of morn, they drift away.
But in the heart, they softly remain,
Whispers of magic, forever gain.

9 781805 633600